American Curl Cats

Stephanie Finne

Checkerboard
Library

An Imprint of Abdo Publishing
www.abdopublishing.com

www.abdopublishing.com

Published by Abdo Publishing, a division of ABDO, PO Box 398166, Minneapolis, Minnesota 55439.
Copyright © 2015 by Abdo Consulting Group, Inc. International copyrights reserved in all countries.
No part of this book may be reproduced in any form without written permission from the publisher.
Checkerboard Library™ is a trademark and logo of Abdo Publishing.

Printed in the United States of America, North Mankato, Minnesota.
032014
092014

THIS BOOK CONTAINS
RECYCLED MATERIALS

Cover Photo: Photo by Helmi Flick
Interior Photos: Alamy p. 5; Glow Images p. 19; Photos by Helmi Flick pp. 9, 13, 21;
    Thinkstock pp. 1, 6–7, 10–11, 14–15, 16, 17

Series Coordinator: Bridget O'Brien
Editors: Rochelle Baltzer, Tamara L. Britton, Megan M. Gunderson
Art Direction: Renée LaViolette

Library of Congress Cataloging-in-Publication Data

Finne, Stephanie, author.
  American curl cats / Stephanie Finne.
     pages cm. -- (Cats)
  Audience: Ages 8-12.
  Includes index.
  ISBN 978-1-62403-321-6
 1. American curl cat--Juvenile literature. 2. Cats--Juvenile literature. I. Title.
  SF449.A44F56 2015
  636.8'3--dc23
                    2013047193

Contents

Lions, Tigers, and Cats

Wild cats have been around for thousands of years. Scientists believe the first ancestor of the cat was a weasel-like animal called Miacis. It lived 40 to 50 million years ago!

Over time, the Miacis developed into the lions, tigers, pumas, and **domestic** cats we see today. Because of this, all modern cats belong to the family **Felidae**.

Wild cats are known for their hunting abilities. So more than 3,500 years ago, humans began taming cats for their hunting skills. The ability to hunt **rodents** and keep grain free from pests made these cats valuable.

Today, there are more than 40 different cat **breeds**. Some look and act like their wild cousins. Others, like the American curl cat, have **unique** features that set them apart.

Today, Americans keep more than 70 million pet cats. The American curl cat is a popular choice.

American Curl Cats

American curl cats aren't just **unique**, they're a new **breed**! In June 1981, Joe and Grace Ruga discovered a pair of kittens outside their California home. They took the kittens in and named them Shulamith and Panda. Within two weeks, Panda disappeared. But Shulamith became a member of the Ruga family.

In December, Shulamith had a **litter** of kittens. Two of the four kittens had curled ears like their mother. The Rugas realized they may have discovered a new breed of cat. They called two well-known **geneticists** to look into this.

After more research and test breeding, a **Cat Fanciers' Association (CFA)** judge was contacted.

The judge said Shulamith would be a candidate as a new **breed**. But he warned it was difficult to be accepted to the **CFA**. It could take a long time.

Yet in 1983, the first American curl was shown at a CFA cat show. It would be just three more years before the breed was accepted for CFA registration. In 1993, the curl advanced to championship status.

American curl cats enjoyed the fastest CFA acceptance of any breed!

Qualities

American curl cats are playful and curious. They keep a kitten-like personality even as they age. Because of this, they are often called the Peter Pan of cats. It's like they never grow up!

American curl cats make great family pets. They are gentle, affectionate, and faithful. This makes them good with children and other pets. Some say they are like dogs because they will follow their owners around. They don't want to miss anything!

American curls will pat their owners to get attention. This **breed** is not very talkative. But, American curls make chirping sounds when they are curious. They are fascinated by water, television, and elevated sleeping areas.

These intelligent, even-tempered cats want to be with their humans at all times.

Coat and Color

American curl cats were the first **breed** to be recognized by the **CFA** as one breed with two coats. Both long and short coats are soft and silky and lie close to the body. The long-haired American curl has a full, **plumed** tail. The tail of a short-haired curl has the same length coat as the rest of its body.

The American curl's coat has two layers. The undercoat keeps the cat warm. The outer coat keeps out water. American curl cats have very little undercoat. This breed does not **shed** very much. So, it does not need much grooming.

Long or short, the coats of American curls come in any color. They also come in many patterns. They can be solid, shaded, smoke, tabby, **bicolor**, **parti-color**, or **pointed**. No matter what color or pattern, the American curl cat is elegant and beautiful.

Like its fur, the American curl's eyes can be any color.

Size

Owners love the American curl's silky coat, but the cat's main feature is its curved ears! These **unique** ears sit on the top of the head. They are wide at the base and curve back in a smooth arc at the tip. Long tufts of hair add to the curve, giving the American curl an alert, perky look.

The American curl has a wedge-shaped head. It features a rounded **muzzle**, straight nose, and walnut-shaped eyes. The tail is about as long as the cat's medium-sized body. It is wide at the base and tapers to a thin tip. The legs are medium length and end in rounded paws.

The American curl's legs support its slender, rectangular body. Females often weigh five to eight pounds (2 to 4 kg). Males are slightly larger at seven to ten pounds (3 to 5 kg).

Not all American curls have curly ears. Some are born with straight ears!

Care

American curl cats are easy to care for. However, they do need regular checkups with a veterinarian. The vet can **spay** or **neuter** cats that will not be **bred**. The cat can also receive **vaccines** during its exam.

Like its wild cat relatives, your cat will need to bury its waste. So, you will need to provide a **litter box**. Make sure to clean it out every day. Cats need to scratch, too! A scratching post will save your furniture from your pet's claws. Give your playful curl toys to entertain itself and keep it out of trouble.

Finally, you will need to give your American curl lots of attention. This breed is active and can be demanding. But, it is also loving and friendly. Playing with your American curl will keep it happy and healthy.

Feeding

Besides love and attention, your American curl cat needs the right diet to stay healthy. Like all cats, American curls need a balanced diet with protein. Choose a food that is labeled "complete and balanced." This means it contains all the **nutrients** your cat needs.

There are different types of food to choose from. Dry foods are less expensive. They also help clean your cat's teeth. Semimoist foods are another option. These foods do not need to be refrigerated. Canned foods are also available. But, they spoil quickly.

Your cat can be fed in one of three ways. It can be portion fed, which means a meal is measured out. It can be time fed, where a cat eats at specific times of day. Or, a cat can be free-choice fed. With this type of feeding, food is always available.

You can discuss feeding options with your vet. No matter how you choose to feed your cat, be sure it always has fresh water.

Kittens need more protein in their diets than adult cats do.

Kittens

Cats are ready to mate when they are 7 to 12 months old. A female cat is **pregnant** for about 65 days. When a cat gives birth, it is called kittening. There are usually four kittens per **litter**.

American curl cats are born with straight ears. In three to five days, the ears start to curl backward. But, they aren't fully curled until the kitten is 16 weeks old.

Kittens are born blind, deaf, and helpless. Their mother watches them closely. After 10 to 12 days, they have developed their senses. They also have teeth. At three weeks, they can walk around and begin exploring their world.

Kittens will drink their mother's milk for about five weeks. Then, they are **weaned** onto solid food. The kittens spend several more weeks learning and growing with their mother. They are ready to be adopted once they are 12 to 16 weeks old.

When they are born, all kittens have blue eyes. After several months, their eyes change to their permanent color.

Buying a Kitten

American curl cats are active and demand a lot of attention. They follow their humans because they like to be involved in everything their owners are doing. So if you want to adopt a curl, be sure you can give it a lot of time.

If you decide to bring home an American curl cat, find a reputable **breeder**. Good breeders know the history of their cats. They sell healthy cats that have had **vaccines**.

Before bringing your cat home, be sure to get some supplies. Food and water dishes, food, a **litter box**, and a cat bed are a good start. Find a local veterinarian who has worked with American curl cats. Then, you will be ready for your new family member!

Most domestic cats will live for 10 to 15 years. But, the oldest cat on record was 34 years old!

Glossary

bicolor - having two colors.

breed - a group of animals sharing the same ancestors and appearance. A breeder is a person who raises animals. Raising animals is often called breeding them.

Cat Fanciers' Association (CFA) - a group that sets the standards for judging all breeds of cats.

domestic - tame, especially relating to animals.

Felidae (FEHL-uh-dee) - the scientific Latin name for the cat family. Members of this family are called felids. They include lions, tigers, leopards, jaguars, cougars, wildcats, lynx, cheetahs, and domestic cats.

gencticist - a scientist who studies genetics. Genetics is a branch of biology that deals with inherited features.

litter - all of the kittens born at one time to a mother cat.

litter box - a box filled with cat litter, which is similar to sand. Cats use litter boxes to bury their waste.

muzzle - an animal's nose and jaws.

neuter (NOO-tuhr) - to remove a male animal's reproductive glands.

nutrient - a substance found in food and used in the body. It promotes growth, maintenance, and repair.

parti-color - having a dominant color broken up by patches of one or more other colors.

plumed - relating to a large, showy feather or something that resembles one.

pointed - having color on the head, paws, and tail.

pregnant - having one or more babies growing within the body.

rodent - any of several related animals that have large front teeth for gnawing. Common rodents include mice, squirrels, and beavers.

shed - to cast off hair, feathers, skin, or other coverings or parts by a natural process.

spay - to remove a female animal's reproductive organs.

unique (yoo-NEEK) - being the only one of its kind.

vaccine (vak-SEEN) - a shot given to prevent illness or disease.

wean - to accustom an animal to eating food other than its mother's milk.

Websites

To learn more about Cats,
visit **booklinks.abdopublishing.com**. These links are routinely monitored and updated to provide the most current information available.

Index